AN ADDRESS

BEFORE THE

VERMONT HISTORICAL SOCIETY.

BY DANIEL P. THOMPSON.

AN

ADDRESS

PRONOUNCED IN THE

REPRESENTATIVES' HALL, MONTPELIER,

24th OCTOBER, 1850,

BEFORE THE

VERMONT HISTORICAL SOCIETY,

IN THE PRESENCE OF

BOTH HOUSES OF THE GENERAL ASSEMBLY;

BY

DANIEL P. THOMPSON.

Published by Order of the Legislature.

BURLINGTON:

FREE PRESS OFFICE PRINT

1850.

Office of the Secretary of the Senate,
Montpelier, Vt., Oct. 29, 1850.

Hon. Daniel P. Thompson, Montpelier.

Sir: We have the pleasure to communicate to you the following resolution, adopted on the 25th inst:—

"Resolved, by the Senate and House of Representatives:

"That the Secretary of the Senate, and the Clerk of the House of "Representatives be instructed to solicit from the Hon. Daniel P. Thomp- "son a copy of the interesting and valuable Address pronounced by him "before the Vermont Historical Society, in presence of the two Houses, "on the evening of the 24th inst., and that the Secretary and Clerk procure "two thousand copies thereof to be printed, and distributed under the di- "rection of His Excellency, the Governor."

We take occasion to express the hope that you will comply with the unanimous desire of the two Houses, in which the entire audience, on the occasion alluded to, participated.

Very respectfully, Your ob't serv'ts,

D. W. C. CLARKE, Secretary of the Senate,

C. F. DAVEY, of the House of Representatives.

Montpelier, Vt., 30th October, 1850.

Gentlemen:

It was not my intention to publish the Address, of which the two Houses have taken such flattering notice, as I thought of embodying it, with further amplifications of the subject, in a work I have in preparation for the press. But perceiving no valid objections to its publication in this form, though it may soon substantially appear in another, and being anxious to make every consistent response to a demonstration, of which I fear neither myself, nor my imperfect effort, is worthy, I can do no less than comply with your request, and that which seems involved in the resolution, a copy of which you have forwarded to me. I, therefore, place the manuscript at your disposal, and, with the assurance of my personal regard, remain

Your friend and ob't serv't,

D. P. THOMPSON.

To Gen. D. W. C. Clarke, Secretary of the Senate,
Chalon F. Davey, Esq., Clerk of the House of Representatives.

ADDRESS.

MR. PRESIDENT AND GENTLEMEN OF THE SENATE AND HOUSE OF REPRESENTATIVES:

VERMONT was ushered into political existence midst storm and tempest. We speak both metaphorically and literally: For it is a curious historical fact that her Constitution, the result of the first regular movement ever made by her people towards an independent civil government, was adopted during the darkest period of the Revolution—at an hour of commotion and alarm, when the tempest of war was actually bursting over her borders and threatening her entire subversion. And, as if to make the event the more remarkable, the adoption took place amidst one of the most memorable thunder storms ever known in Vermont, but for the providential occurrence of which, at that particular juncture, that important political measure, as we shall soon make apparent, must have been postponed to an indefinite period, and what is more, to a period when the growing dissensions, which, as soon as the common danger was over, New York and New Hampshire contrived to scatter among her people, must have defeated it, and thus destroyed all their prospects of the blessings of an independent civil government forever.

The whole history of the settlement and organization of this State, indeed, exhibits, when compared with those of another, the most striking anomaly. She may emphatically be called the offspring of war and controversy. The long and fierce dispute for territory between the colonies just named, had sown her soil with Dragon teeth, which at length sprang up in a crop of hardy, determined, and liberty-loving men, who instead of joining either of the contending parties, soon resolved to take a stand for themselves against both. And that stand they maintained with a spirit and success, to which, considering the discouragements, difficulties and dangers they were constantly compelled to encounter, history scarcely furnishes a parallel. But though every step of her progress, from the felling of the first tree in her dark wilderness to her final reception into the sisterhood of the States, was marked by the severest trials, yet the memorable year of '77, was incomparably the most trying and gloomy as well as the most glorious of her history. Within a period of forty days, indeed, from the first landing of the vauntful Burgoyne on her shores at Ticonderoga, on the 6th of July, to the 16th of August, when his Lion Flag was seen trailing in the dust at Bennington, her whole destinies seemed crowded; but it was in those very days of darkness and dismay, that she settled them all, and ensured her independence forever!

Conceiving this eventful period, therefore, to be the turning point in the destinies of Vermont, as a separate State, we shall confine our remarks to this important part of her history, and endeavor to unfold the secret and hitherto little known, but, in our estimation, the main springs of action, by which such momentous results were accomplished.

In the beginning of this memorable year the people of Vermont by their delegates in formal Convention assembled had declared themselves Independent,

"Independent of all save the mercies of God,"

to use the significant language which the poet has put into the mouth of one of their numbers. And having taken measures for publishing their declaration to the world, this Convention closed its proceedings by appointing a committee to draft a Constitution to be submitted to a new Convention which the people were invited to call for the purpose. In response to that call, a new Convention assembled at Windsor about the first of July following, and proceeded, with that dilligence and scrupulous regard to the employment of their time, for which our *earlier* public bodies were noted, to take into consideration the important instrument now submitted to them as a proper basis, on which to erect the superstructure of a civil government suited to the genius and necessities of an industrious an frugal people—a people who, though keenly jealous of their individual rights, and exceedingly restive under all foreign authority, had yet declared the wish to receive and obey a system of legal restraints, if it could be one of their own imposing—a people who had said to their leaders :

> "Tho' we owe no allegiance and bow to no throne,
> We will yield to the law if that law be our own."

For five days, from rising to setting sun, this Convention employed the best energies of their enlightened and practical minds in discussing and amending the document before them. But their labors had well nigh been lost, for the present certainly, and, for reasons before given, probably forever. For soon after they had assembled on the 6th day of their Session, and while they were intently listening to the reading of the instrument for the last time before taking a final vote on its adoption, their proceedings were suddenly brought to a stand by the alarming news, loudly proclaimed from an open despatch from the gallant Warner by a herald who appeared on his foam covered horse before their open door, that Ticonderoga, the supposed inpregnable barrier of frontier defence, had fallen, and our scattered troops were flying in all directions before a formidable British army that was sweeping unopposed along the western border of the State, flanked by a horde of merciless savages, from whose fearful irruptions not a dwelling on that side the mountains would probably be spared! This intelligence, so unexpected and so startling, too nearly concerned the members of this body as men as well as patriots, to permit their entire exemption from the general feeling of consternation and dismay which was everywhere spreading, on the wings of the wind, around them; and many a staid heart among them secretly trembled for the fate of the near and dear ones left at home, in which the red tomahawk might, even at that moment be busy at its work of death; while the bosoms of all were burning to seize the sword or musket and fly to their relief or mingle in the common defence of their endangered country. Any further proceedings with the subject on hand, at such a moment was soon found to be impossible, and the greater number began to clamor for an immediate adjournment. But while a few, who had shared less than others in the panic, or were more deeply impressed with the importance of accomplishing an object, at this time, now so nearly attained, were vainly attempting to resist the current, till time was gained for reflection, an unwonted darkness, as if by special interposition of Providence, fell suddenly upon the earth. The lightnings began to gleam through the dark and threatening masses of clouds that had enveloped the sky, and the long, deep roll of thunder was heard in every quarter of the heavens, giving warning of the severe and protracted tempest, which now soon burst over them with a fury that precluded all thought of venturing abroad. The prospect of being thus confined to the place for some hours, if not for the whole day, taking from the movers all inducement for immediate adjournment, they now began to take a cooler view of the subject; and soon, by common consent, the business on hand was resumed. The reading of the Constitution was finished, and, while the storm was still howling around them, and the thunders breaking over their heads, that instrument was adopted and became the supreme law of the land.* One thing more, however, remained to be done; and that was to constitute a provisional government to act till the one pointed out by the Constitution could be established. This was now effected by the appointment of that small body of men, 13 in number, it is believed, since known as THE OLD COUNCIL OF SAFETY OF VERMONT, and noted alike for the remarkable powers with which they were invested, and the remarkable manner in which those powers were exercised: For from the

*This Constitution was never submitted to the people fo rratification, but by general consent acquiesced in without that usual formality.

nature of the case, and the emergency in which these men were called to act, they were almost necessarily invested with the extraordinary combination of legislation, Judicial and Executive power. But this power, absolute and dictatorial as it was, they never abused, nor exercised but for the public good, and in this they were cheerfully sustained by the people, who felt that they were thus not only sustaining the cause of Freedom, but the laws which were of their own providing, and which they were now anxious should be strictly obeyed.*

To that unique assembly, whose origin we have just described, we now propose to introduce our auditors at its most interesting and important session. In obedience to the order of the Convention, they had promptly assembled at Manchester, and here, conscious that the eyes of all were turned anxiously upon them in expectation that they would provide for the safety of their infant State, whose now fearfully menaced destinies had been committed into their hands, they commenced the worse than Egyptian task devolving on them—that of making adequate provisions for the public defence, while the means were almost wholly wanting. For with scarcely the visible means in the whole settlement, in its then exhausted and unsettled condition, of raising and supporting a single company of soldiers, they were expected to raise an army; without the shadow of a public Treasury, and without any credit as a State, and without the power of taxing the people, which, by the Constitution just adopted, could only be done by a legislature not yet called, they were required to do that for which half a million was needed. Such were the difficulties by which they were met at the outset—difficulties, which, to men of ordinary stamina and mental resources, would have been insurmountable. But the members of the Old

*The council of safety continued to exercise all these powers till March 1778, when it was superceded by the legislature, then first convening, in all its civil functions, while those relating to war were transferred to a new body appointed by the legislature, called the Board of War.

Council of Safety were not men of ordinary stamina, either moral or mental, and the results of their action amid all these difficulties and discouragements were soon to evince it to the world. The particular time however, we have chosen for lifting the curtain from their secret proceedings, was at the darkest, and most disheartening hour they were doomed to experience, and before their united mind had been brought to bear on any measure affording the least promise of auspicious results. The army of Burgoyne was then hovering on their borders in its most menacing attitude. Marauding parties were daily penetrating the interior, plundering and capturing the defenceless inhabitants ; while each day brought the unwelcome news of the defection of individuals who had gone off to swell the ranks of the victorious enemy, to whose alarming progress scarcely a show of resistance had yet been interposed. Nor was this the end of the chapter of the trials that awaited them. Another blow was to be added, more calculated than all to test their firmness and bring home to their bosoms a sense of the perils of the crisis, and the necessity of prompt action, unless they should conclude to give up and yield unresistingly to the current of destiny that seemed to be setting so strongly against them. But let us now present the mortifying event to which we have just alluded in another form, together with the action that followed, and personal descriptions of the actors, gathered from the writings left by one of their number,* from the lips of old men now passed away, and especially of one whom this year has numbered with the dead and who, then an observant boy,† was permitted to be an eye and ear witness of all that occurred in the debate which we will try to bring up as a living and truthful picture directly to the senses :—

The long summer day was drawing to a close. It had been thus far spent by the Council, as had been several of the preceding, in discussing the ways and means for doing something

*Ira Allen—see appendix.
†Daniel Chipman.

to avert the doom that hung over their seemingly devoted State. But up to this hour their deliberations had been wholly fruitless. Project after project for raising military forces had been brought forward, discussed and abandoned, as impracticable, till wearied with the unavailing labors, and disheartened by the dismal prospect before them, they were about to give up business for the day when the door-keeper, with unwonted haste and an agitated manner, entered the room, and announced to the astonished members the alarming tidings that one of their own number, and till that day an active participator in their discussions, had proved a Judas, and was now, with a band of his recreant neighbors, on his way to the British camp ! This news fell like a thunder-clap on the Council, producing at first a sensation not often witnessed in so grave an assemblage. But no formal comments were offered, and, after the commotion had subsided, all sank into a thoughtful silence, which we will improve by personal introductions of all the leading members of this body, whom we are now to suppose sitting before us digesting the tidings just announced.

Separated from the rest by a sort of enclosure composed of tables strung across one end of the apartment, which was the large upper room of the old tavern in Manchester, and which had been hastily fitted up for the occasion, sat the President of the Council—the venerable THOMAS CHITTENDEN, the wise, the prudent and the good, who was to Vermont what Washington was to the whole country, and who, though possessing no dazzling greatness, had yet that rare combination of moral and intellectual qualities which was far better—good sense, great discretion, honesty of purpose, and an unvarying equanimity of temper, united with a modest and pleasing address. And by the long and continued exercise of this golden mean of qualities, he was destined to leave behind him, an honest and enduring fame—a memorial of good deeds and useful every-day examples to be remembered and quoted both in the domestic circle and public assembly, when the superior brilliancy of many a cotemporary had passed away and been forgotten. He was now over fifty, but so fine his physical endowments, and so good his habits, that time had left scarcely a trace on his manly brow; and notwithstanding the simplicity of his deportment and the plainness of his dress, the large arm chair in which he was reclining, furnished by some considerate matron of the neighborhood, could not have found, in the broad land, an occupant who would have filled it with more native dignity, or one better fitted to restrain by courteous firmness, and by tact guide into safe and appropriate fields of action, the less diciplined and more fiery spirits of the body over whom he presided.

On the left of the President, on one of the plain benches that ran along the walls in front, immersed in thought, sat side by side, like brothers as they were, the two FAYS—those intelligent and persevering friends of freedom and State independence. Further along sat the two ROBINSONS, alike patriotic and active or able, according to the different spheres in which they were about to be distinguished—one in the tented field, and the other on the Bench, and in the Councils of the Nation. Next to them was seen the short, burly form of the uncompromising MATTHEW LYON, the Irish refugee, who was willing to be sold, as he was, to pay his passage, for a pair of two-year-old bulls, by which he was wont to swear on all extra occasions—thus sold for the sake of getting out of the king-tainted atmosphere of the old world, into one where his broad chest could expand freely, and his bold, free spirit soar untrammeled by the clogs of legitimacy. In his eagle eye, and every lineament of his clear, ardent and fearless countenance, might be read the promise of what he was to become—the stern Democrat, and unflinching champion of the whole right and the largest liberty.

In contrast to him, on the opposite side, was seen the tall form, and the firm and thoughtful countenance of BENJAMIN CARPENTER, who, by his line of marked trees through a 30-mile reach of woods, had just arrived on foot with pack and cane, from his residence in Guilford, on the other side of the mountains.

Next sat the mild and gentlemanly NATHAN CLARK, the future Speaker of the Legislature ; and by his side the dark, rough featured GIDEON OLIN, another embryo member of Congress, knitting his brows in an expression of mingled sternness and gloom.

Beyond these, leaning out of an open window, was THOMAS ROWLEY, the first Poet of the Green Mountains. He was here because he was a public favorite, a trusty patriot, and something of a statesman. But like other poets he had his peculiar temperament, as might be seen even in this staid assembly. For, as if disgusted with a profitless debate, and determined not to be troubled by the disconcerting news just announced, he had turned to the more congenial employment of gazing out on the landscape, over which his kindling eye might have been seen to wander, till it rested in rapture on the broad empurpled side and bright summit of the lofty Equinox mountain, whose contrasted magnificence was growing every moment more striking and beautiful in the beams of the setting sun.

At an end of one of the tables before the President, was also seen the stout frame and business like countenance of PAUL SPOONER, engaged in writing a despatch. And as the last, though not as the least of this contrasted assemblage, let us turn to the youthful Secretary of the Council, IRA ALLEN. So much the junior of his colleagues was he, that a spectator might well wonder why he was selected as one of such a sage body. But those who procured his appointment knew full well why they had done so ; and his history thenceforward was destined to prove a continued justification of their opinion. Both in form and feature, he was one of the handsomest men of his day ; while a mind, at once versatile, clear and penetrating, with perceptions as quick as light, was stamped on his Grecian brow, or found a livelier expression in his flashing black eyes and other lineaments of his intellectual countenance. Such, as he appeared for the first time on the stage of public action, was the afterwards noted Ira Allen, whose true history, when written, will show him to have been either secretly or openly the originator or successful prosecutor of more important political measures, affecting the interests and independence of the State, and the issue of the war in the Northern department, than any other individual in Vermont; making him, with the many peculiar traits he possessed, one of the most remarkable men of the times in which he so conspicuously figured.

"I have finished," said Spooner, breaking the gloomy silence which had so long pervaded the assembly,—"I have finished the despatch, Mr. President, requiring the attendance of Gen. Bailey, the absent member from Newbury, and I have ventured to add the news of the defection of that miserable Squire Spencer!"*

"Tis all well," responded the President; "but I had hoped to have forwarded by the same messenger, a despatch requesting the aid of New Hampshire. But how can we expect they will do anything till we do something for ourselves—till they know whether they will find among us more friends to feed and assist, than enemies to impede them. And I submit to you, gentlemen, whether it is not now high time to act to some purpose. If we can't vote taxes, we can contribute towards raising a military force if you will agree to raise one. Instead of being disheartened by the conduct of the traitor Spencer, who has perhaps providentially left us before we had settled on any plan of operations which he could report to the enemy, let us show him, and the world, that the rest of us can be *men!* I have ten head of cattle which, by way of example, I will give for the emergency. But am I more patriotic than the rest of you here, and hundreds of others in the settlement? My wife has a valuable gold necklace; hint to her to-day that it is needed, and my word for it, to-morrow will find it in the treasury of freedom. But is my wife more spirited than yours and others? Gentlemen, I wait your propositions."

---

*See Appendix.

During this effective appeal, drooping heads began to be raised—perplexed countenances began to brighten, and by the time he had closed, several speakers were on their feet eager to respond.

"Mr. Carpenter has the floor, gentlemen," said the President, evidently wishing that discreet and firm man should lead off as a sort of guide to the warm emotions he saw rising.

"I rose," said Carpenter, "to give my hearty response to the sentiments of the Chair. It *is* time, *high* time to act. I have no definite proposition now to offer; but within one hour, I *will* have one, if others are not before me in the matter. For it is a *crime* to dally any longer, and from this moment action shall be my motto."

"Aye, action! action! responded several.

"Action let it be, then," said the impulsive Rowley, the next to speak; "and I will make a proposition, that will give gentlemen all the action they will want, besides setting an example which will show *works* as well as faith—I propose, Mr. President, that each one of us here, before any more of us run away to the enemy, seize a standard,—repair singly to the different hamlets among our mountains—cause the summoning drum to be beat for volunteers, whom we will *ourselves* lead to do battle with this Jupiter Olympus of a British General, who has so nearly annihilated us by force of Proclamation!"

"Tom Rowley all over! but a gallant push nevertheless," exclaimed Samuel Robinson in an under tone, "and yet Mr. President," he continued rising, "if our spirited colleague's proposal should be carried into effect, we should still want a regularly enlisted force to serve as a nucleus to volunteers, especially under such officers as most of us would make. I therefore move we vote to raise a company of an hundred men, which will be as many as all the contributions we can obtain among our poor and distressed people, will equip and support very long in the field."

"And I," said Clark, "believing we may venture to go a little higher than that, propose to raise two companies of sixty each."

"No, no," cried several voices. "One company—means can be found for no more."

"Yes, yes, the larger number—I go for two companies," cried others.

"And I go for neither, Mr. President," said Ira Allen, dashing down his pen upon the table, by the side of which he had been sitting in deep cogitation. "I have heard all the propositions yet advanced—see the difficulties of all, and yet I see a way by which we can do something more worthy the character of the Green Mountain Boys—and that too without infringing the Constitution or distressing the people. I therefore move, Sir, that this Council resolve to raise a whole regiment of men, appoint their officers, and take such prompt measures for their enlistment, that within one week every glen in our mountains shall resound with the din of military preparations."

"Chimerical!" said one who, in common with the rest of the Council, seemed to hear with much surprise a proposition of such magnitude so confidently put forth, when the general doubt appeared to be whether even the comparatively trifling one of Clark should be adopted.

"Impossible—utterly impossible to raise pay for half of them," exclaimed others.

"Don't let us say that, till compelled to," said Carpenter in an encouraging tone. "Though I don't now see where the means are to come from, yet new light may break in on us by another day, so that we can see our way clear to sustain this proposition. If there should, we should feel like *men* again."

"Amen to all that," responded Clark, "and as the hour of adjournment has arrived, I move that our young colleague who seems so confident in the matter of means, be a committee of one, to devise those ways and means to pay the bounties and wages of the regiment he proposes, and that he make his report thereof by sunrise to-morrow morning."

"I second that motion, so plase ye, Mr. President," cried Lyon in his usual full determined tone and Irish accent—"I go for Mr. Allen's proposition entirely, manes or no manes. But the manes must and shall be found. We will put the brave gentleman's brains under the screw to-night," he added jocosely, "and if he appears empty handed in the morning, he ought to be expelled from the Council. Aye, and I'll move it too, by the two bulls that redamed me!"

"I accept the terms!" said Allen—"give me a room by myself, pen, ink, paper and candles, and I will abide the condition."

"For your light, Mr. Allen, as your task is to find money where there is none to any common view, I would advise you to borrow the wonderful lamp of Aladdin," gaily added Rowley, as the Council broke up and separated for the night.

At sunrise the next morning all the Council were in their seats to receive the promised report. They were aware that Allen had spent the whole night on the business committed to his charge; for, hour after hour during that important night, they had heard the alternate scratching of his rapid pen, and the sound of his footsteps as he paced his solitary chamber, intensely revolving in his teeming mind the details of a plan, on the success of which with the Council he felt the last chance of making a stand against the invaders of the State must depend. This circumstance, together with the expectation which his confident manner, and known fertility in expedients had previously created, that he would present some feasible plan for carrying out his proposal, though no one could conjecture its character, now caused his appearance to be awaited with no little curiosity and solicitude.—They were not long kept in suspense. Allen, with his papers in hand, came in, and after announcing his readiness to report, calmly proceeded to unfold his plan, which was nothing more nor less than the bold and undreamed-of step of confiscating, seizing and, on the shortest legal notice, selling at the post, the estate of every Tory in Vermont, for the public service!

The speaker having read his report, consisting of a decree of confiscation, drawn up ready for adoption by the Council, and a list of candidates or nominations of officers for a regiment of Rangers, he quickly resumed his seat and patiently awaited the action of the Council. But they were taken by such complete surprise by a proposition, at that time so new in the colonies, so bold and so startling in its character, that, for many minutes, not a word or whisper was heard through the hushed assembly, whose bowed heads and working countenances showed how intensely their minds were engaged in trying to grapple with the subject matter on which their action was so unexpectedly required.

Soon, however, low murmurs of doubt or disapproval began to be heard, and the expressions—*Unprecedented step! Doubtful policy! Injury to the cause!* became distinguishable among the more timid in different parts of the room, when the prompt and fearless Matthew Lyon, whose peculiar traits of intellect had made him the first to meet and master the proposition, which jumped so well with his feelings, and whose consequent resolve to support it was only strengthened by the tokens of rising opposition he perceived around him, now sprang to his feet, and, bringing his broad palms together with a loud slap, exultingly exclaimed: "The child is born, Mr. President! My head," he continued, "has been in a continual fog, ever since we met, till the present moment. But now, thank God, I can see my way out of it,—I can now see at a glance how all we want, can be readily—aye, and righteously, accomplished! I can already see a regiment of our brave mountaineers in arms before me, as the certain fruits of this bold, bright thought of our young friend here.

"*Unprecedented step* is it? It may be so with us timid Republicans; but is it so with our enemies, who are this moment threatening to crush us, because we object to receive their law and precedent? How, in Heaven's name, were they to obtain the lands of half Vermont, which they offered the lion-hearted Ethan Allen if he would join them, but by confiscating *our* estates? What became of the estates of those in their country, who, like ourselves, rebelled against their government? Why, sir, they were confiscated! Can *they* complain, then, if we adopt a measure, which, in case we are vanquished, they will visit on *our* estates, to say nothing of our necks? And can these recreant rascals themselves, who have left their property among us, and gone off to help fasten the very law and precedent on us, complain at our doing what they will be the first to recommend to be done to us, if their side prevails? Where, then, is the *doubtful policy* of our anticipating them in the measure, any more than seizing one of their loaded guns in battle and turning it against them?

Injury to the cause, will it be? Will it injure our cause here, where men are daily deserting to the British, in the belief that we shall not dare touch their property, to strike a blow that will deter all the wavering, and most others of any property, from leaving us hereafter? Will it injure our cause here, to have a regiment of regular troops, who will draw into the field four times their numbers of volunteers? If that be an injury, Mr. President, I only wish we had more of them! With half a dozen such injuries, we would rout Burgoyne's whole army in a fortnight. I go, then, for the proposition to the death, Mr. President. Yes, by the two Bulls that redamed me, I will go it!"

The ice was broken. This bold dash of rough, argumentative eloquence, so adroitly addressed to men of such mould, had reached cords that rose responsive to the touch, and gave a direction to the naturally favoring current of their feelings, which was not to be diverted. The more ready and fearless, one after another, now stepped forward, removed obstructions, and gave additional force to the gathering impetus. The President, on whom all eyes were turned, was seen nodding his approbation in spite of all his prudence. The timid rapidly gained strength, the doubters at length yielded, and, within two hours, this all important measure, which, in the eventful period of forty days, named at the outset, became the pivot on which the destinies of Vermont were turned, was unanimously adopted. The results were soon apparent. Doubt and despondency gave place to confidence and courage. Commissioners, and other officers, were appointed and dispatched in every direction to seize the marked estates, and the whole enginery of sequestration was at once put in motion. The work of enlistment under the ardent and active HERRICK and his subordinates, the military appointees of the Council, was commenced; and within one week every village and hamlet in the Green Mountains were resounding with the roll of the recruiting drum, and the clang of war-like preparation.—With such energy and success, indeed, were these operations pushed forward, that within the astonishingly short period of fifteen days, a respectably filled regiment was collected and ready to take the field. All this had led to a confident and successful appeal to New Hampshire, for aid and cooperation. STARK came. The battle of Bennington was fought and won; and the shout of victory, that went up from the banks of the Waloomsic, was a virtual proclamation of the Independence of Vermont.—For, her gallantry here, and her controlling hand in getting up an expedition, resulting so disastrously to Burgoyne—so auspiciously to the country, gave her a right to *command* a boon, which she otherwise would have sued for in vain;—a boon which she *did* thus command, thus receive,—and thus ensure for herself her subsequent proud and happy destiny.

APPENDIX.

Extracts from Ira Allen's history of Vermont, and his address to the Legislature, in relation to a cargo of military stores bought by him in Europe, for the militia of Vermont, and seized by the British;—published in 1808, now nearly out of print:

"The members of the Convention repaired to Windsor, July 4th, 1777. A draft of the Constitution was laid before them and read. The business being new, and of great consequence, required serious deliberation. The Convention had it under consideration, when the news of the evacuation of Ticonderoga arrived, which alarmed them very much, as thereby the Frontiers were exposed to the inroads of the enemy. The family of the President of the Convention, as well as those of many other members, were exposed to the foe. In this awful crisis, some were for leaving precipitately; but a severe thunder-storm came on, and during the rain, they had time to reflect; while other members, less alarmed at the news, called the attention of the whole to finish the Constitution, which was then reading for the last time. The Constitution was read through; the Convention proceeded to appoint a Council of Safety to conduct the business of the State, and adjourned without day." * * * * *

"The members of the Council of Safety, appointed as aforesaid, agreed to meet and form at Manchester, where they repaired without loss of time. Col. Thomas Chittenden was elected President, and Mr. Ira Allen (then 27 years old) Secretary to said Convention." * * * *

"The Council of Safety had no public money, nor had they any authority to lay taxes, or credit as a public body, to make or borrow money to answer the necessities of government. The government was in its infancy, and all expenses were supported at private expense. The Council were generally men of small property, yet in this situation, it became necessary to raise men for the defence of the Frontiers, with bounties and wages. Ways and means were to be found out; and the day was spent in debating on the subject. Nathan Clark, Esq., not convinced of the practicability of raising a regiment, moved in Council, that Mr. Ira Allen, (the youngest member of the Council; who insisted on raising a regiment, while a large majority of the Council were for only two companies of 60 men each) might be appointed a committee, to discover ways and means to raise, arm and support a regiment, and to make his report at sun-rise, on the morrow. The Council acquiesced, and Mr. Allen took the matter into consideration, and spent the night alone in concerting plans; and he reported the ways and means, viz., that the Council should appoint Commissioners of sequestration, with authority to seize the goods and chattels of all persons who had, or should join the common enemy; that all moveable property so seized should be sold at public vendue, and the proceeds paid to a treasurer, to be appointed by the Council, for the purpose of paying a bounty of $10, and one month's pay in advance; that every man furnish his own arms, &c.

The Council appointed Commissioners of sequestration, Ira Allen Treasurer, and the officers for a regiment, (the nomination of which Mr. Allen had paid much attention to in the solitary hours of the night.) Samuel Herrick was appointed Colonel, and the men enlisted and said bounties paid in 15 days, out of the confiscated property of the enemies of the new State. This was (supposed to be) the first instance of seizing and selling the property of the enemies of American Independence."

"Abel Spencer, of Clarendon, who had been a stickler for New York, had been suddenly converted to an advocate for a new State, and so ingratiated himself, as a good whig, that he was elected a member of the Council of Safety. Mr. Allen declared he would not take a seat in the Council if Spencer did, and that he should not be surprised if Spencer should go to Burgoyne's camp; which he did, and died with the British soon after."

An original letter written in Council by Spooner, in which he alludes to Spencer's desertion, is still preserved in the collection of the Historical Society.

Though personal estate was only at first seized, probably to raise money for immediate necessities, yet the confiscation and sale of real estate was either put in train at the same time, or soon after.

www.ingramcontent.com/pod-product-compliance
Lightning Source LLC
LaVergne TN
LVHW011143110826
845150LV00008B/2482

9781418192563